Dear Reader,

Debra began seeing smiles all around her a very long time ago. The intention of this book is for you to begin seeking smiles in your daily life. Or just to enjoy the pictures.

At first, Frank thought finding a smile in an unexpected place was a rarity. Eventually he started seeing them too and they'd amuse each other with the latest find.

According to Wikipedia, Pareidolia is the tendency for perception to impose a meaningful interpretation on a nebulous stimulus, usually visual, so that one sees an object, pattern, or meaning where there is none. It is a type of apophenia. Apophenia is the tendency to perceive meaningful connections between unrelated things.

According to Abe Lincoln "Half the stuff you read on Wikipedia is either misleading or outright wrong. When you think you see a smile, it's a smile!"

Smiles and hugs are two things that are most often returned.

Wishing you love, light, laughter, and smiles : )


Debra & Frank

Life smiles at us all;
all we can do is smile back

Even if you had a bad day.
You can still find a smile!

I'd listen to him;
always smiling and happy!

Yes! Smiles are contagious.
What a difference a smile make

Hahahahaha!
I escaped the Fork Monster

So happy to have made that sauce!
Remember, it's sauce, not gravy.
Gravy is for turkeys.

RAV4
4WD
NEW YORK

A smile? An owl in a tree, or both?

www.ingramcontent.com/pod-product-compliance
Lightning Source LLC
Chambersburg PA
CBRC090747110726
48005CB00008B/991